D1649078

BUSIA

Seasons on the Farm with My Polish Grandmother

Leonard Kniffel

Busia
Copyright 2017 by Leonard Kniffel

Published by PolishSon.com
Chicago, Illinois

Printed in USA by Bookmasters, Ashland, Ohio

Library of Congress Control Number: 2016959480

ISBN 978-0-692-03294-7

For my cousins, in memory of our grandmother,
Helena Bryszkiewska Misiuk Brodacka

Autumn

The year is 1953. Dwight D. Eisenhower is in the first year of his presidency. Picture a farm in Michigan. The suburbs of Detroit have not yet been built. The countryside around the little town called Romeo is a patchwork of fields, stitched together by wire fences and wooden poles. The farm where I lived with Busia, my Polish grandmother, was different from most. Much of the land was in the Soil Bank, a government program that regulated crops by paying farmers not to plant them.

After her husband died in 1950, Busia was never the same. Two years later, she was left alone when the youngest of her seven children, Mary and Hank, married. At the same time, my mother, Lucy, scandalized our Catholic family by leaving her alcoholic, philandering husband. It was determined that I would live with Busia, while my mother rented a tiny apartment in the city and went to work in a bakery in Hamtramck, a Polish enclave surrounded by Detroit. Mama, as I called her, came out to the farm when she could afford the fare for a Greyhound bus ride up Van Dyke Avenue to Romeo, where she was deposited at the Peerless Café to wait for Auntie Louise to pick her up in her green 1949 Plymouth with the tan interior.

In order to buy their own farms and start their own families, Busia's sons Hank and his older brother John had sold the family farm, which they had purchased from the Foote family. It was the last in a long line of farms where my grandparents had been tenant farmers. Uncle Joe, John's twin brother, bought the farm next door after he was disowned by his father for marrying Auntie Louise, who was not Catholic. Stan was Busia's eldest son, and he and her three other boys supplied her principal source of income, most of which she used to pay rent to the new owner so she could continue to live in her own house.

Today, the landlord's pickup truck is rattling up the gravel driveway as it does once a month. Busia and I are in the kitchen listening as the man who owns our house climbs the creaky wooden backporch steps.

"Good morning, Mrs.," he says politely, his singsong accent making it sound as if he is saying "Gouda mourning."

I hide behind the woodpile in the kitchen while Busia stands at the back door and surrenders the four ten-dollar bills she has withdrawn from a cedar box in the top drawer of her oak dresser, where she stores the cash her sons give her for the monthly ritual.

The landlord is a slender, olive-skinned man, who always seems to be in a hurry to leave. "Thank you, Mrs.," he says, stuffing the bills into his baggy coveralls as he descends the porch steps like a timid stick insect. He climbs into the running truck, grinds the gears into reverse, and speeds down the driveway with the crunching sound of heavy rubber tires on pebbles.

At four feet eight inches tall, my grandmother was only a few inches shorter than the landlord, but to me, at the age of six, they were both giants. I remember asking if the landlord was a bad man. "No, Lenuś," Busia answered in broken English, "Is Italian man. He just want his money." Lenuś was her Polish diminutive for my American name, Lennie; it sounded like "Lenoosh." "Busia" was a term of endearment from the Polish word for grandmother, *Babcia*; it sounded like "Boosha."

No one plowed our forty acres in the spring, and no one harvested crops in the fall. Instead of the wheat, corn, and oats it once produced for our family in abundance, the uncultivated ground grew weeds and wildflowers, goldenrod and timothy. The ungrazed pastures produced daisies and milkweed and Queen Anne's lace. Cows no longer ambled along the creek bank, so wild irises and violets grew there in lush blue and purple clusters.

No one used the buildings on the farm except me, and I found in each the peculiar leftovers of another time. The barn contained musty, graying stacks of baled hay in a haymow that was once filled to the top

2

with every summer's sweet-smelling clover and alfalfa. Dust and cob-webs decorated the stanchions where, many years before, the cows had slogged their way from the lane to be milked.

Next to the barn, and sided with the same weathered boards, was the chicken coop, now a storage place for the landlord's lumber. The pig-pen, adjacent to the chicken coop, was home for the wreckage of an old green-fendered tractor that Uncle Stan called a "doodlebug." Between the pen and the coop was a wooden fence, over which we pitched our old tin cans and empty jars.

Closer to the house was a garage and a building divided in two by a thick wall; one part was the old milk house, the other part was the coal bin. Once a year a big dirty truck unloaded a winter's supply of the combustible black stone, which we burned in the coal stove that warmed us from its place in the dining room at the center of our unin-sulated ten-room farmhouse.

Except for the landlord's monthly intrusions, it seemed to me that the farm belonged to me and my grandmother. I played wherever I chose, alone. There was the rope swing in the deserted barn. Busia had no car and would not know how to drive one if she did, so the garage housed dozens of old tools—hoes, rakes, shovels, scythes, and cigar boxes of carefully sorted screws and nails and nuts and bolts that Dziadzia, my grandfather, had saved over his lifetime. I climbed on board the old tractor in the pigpen, as I called my grandfather, and pretended I was driving. When the creek froze solid, I slid on the ice and dived into the snowdrifts shaped by the wind that swept across the fields.

Every day, I packed the woodbox with dry sticks and splintered boards. From inside the house, Busia could reach inside and take out kindling to start a fire in the morning and bring the kitchen stove to just the right temperature for baking. At six, I was big for my age and strong, "growing like a weed," as my mother said. "You need to go to school next year before the truant officer comes after us." And so I would, reluc-tantly, enter first grade a year older and a foot taller than everyone else.

When dusk came, it was my job to stack logs beside the big stove in the dining room and put coal in the pail. Coal was expensive, and we used it sparingly to keep the fire burning all night in the dining room. Wood was free; every year Uncle Hank brought a truckload from the woods on his new farm.

Today, not long after the landlord has left, it is already dark outside, and I have forgotten to fill the coal pail. Busia sits in her chair and rocks as she works a long steel hook around inch after inch of rag strips that she has cut from old clothes and sewed together. Magically the old shirts and dresses became circles in a thick, colorful new rug. Uncle John fashioned the hook for her from a steel rod. "Here Ma, I made this for you," he said when he handed it to her after she broke her last wooden rug hook. "Unbreakable. You'll never need another one."

"Lenuś, I think maybe you should go get it more coal before go to bed, so fire no go out by morning," Busia says. I don't like the dark walk alone into the pitch blackness of the coal bin. In the daytime, the bin seemed harmless and near; at night, the same journey seemed to take forever.

I secure the snaps on my red wool coat, pick up the coal pail, and speed out the back door. The wooden screen door slap shut behind me.

"I'll be right back," I call, waiting to hear the reassuring sound of my grandmother's voice.

"No fall down," she sings after me.

The porch light brightens parts of the path to the coal bin, but in every other direction is what seems like unlimited darkness— without houses or cars or other people. Leaving footprints in the frost, I round the corner of the house, out of the porch light's beam, and rush to the coal bin door, set down the pail, undo the latch, and flip the switch inside the bin. A bare light bulb dangles among the baskets stored in the rafters, making shadows dance in bizarre shapes over the walls. The leafless bushes outside the bin scratch at the building. The small dirty window at the end of the shed flickers with Jack Frost's eerie handiwork.

Four scoops fill the pail with as much coal as I can carry. I throw down the shovel, dash to the door, and flip off the light switch.

Everything is black again; the sounds are still there—the scratching, the wind, the creaking, the vast, dark emptiness. I run up the porch steps, grab the rickety doorknob, and shake it until the door flies open.

Inside the house, I set down the pail and lock the door behind me—the end of a cold-weather ritual that I had performed for as long as I was old enough to carry the pail.

Busia looks up from her rug. "Why you run so hard?" she asks, smiling her toothless smile and tucking a wisp of gray hair behind her ear.

"It's cold outside," I lie, hiding my fright and changing the subject. "What are those baskets for?" "Baskets for funeral," Busia says, as her rug hook starts moving again in her nimble fingers.

In the old farmhouse, I slept in the dining room behind the stove. The next room was Busia's bedroom. It was cold and she slept under an old duvet, her *pierzyna* in Polish, made from goose feathers that she had plucked long ago from the birds before preparing them for dinner. The parlor and the living room were closed off for the winter with heavy drapes and blankets to hold in the heat. Behind them was the old brown mohair davenport and matching chair and the furniture my mother made her brothers bring to the farm when her husband threatened to sell it all. Especially prized was her "Duncanfied" table, as she called the Duncan Phyfe mahogany dining room set that she displayed proudly in front of the double window swathed in Priscilla curtains, which required an entire day to wash and iron. The parlor contained a cast iron bed, the one Dziadzia died in when I was three. Five bedrooms upstairs were behind a door that would seldom be opened until spring.

I had only two memories of Dziadzia, one at his wake when his body was laid out in the parlor and my mother and Auntie Mary were crying because I asked them when he was going to get up. The other was of him tinkering in the garage and laughing when I closed the door and told him he was locked in. Busia never talked about him, but his children, especially my mother, would later tell me stories about how mean and miserable he was, saying little, showing his children no affection but barking out orders, "Go milk the cows!"

The wood in the stove blazes, igniting the coals for the long night ahead. I hurry into my flannel pajamas and jump into bed, curling myself into a ball between the cold sheets. I can hear Busia through the wall, shuffling around in her bedroom, getting into her long flannel nightgown. Then she is silent, and I know she is reading from her prayer book, as she does every night. That reminds me that I have not said my own prayers. Jumping from bed and to my knees, I recite "The Lord's Prayer" as fast as I can, finishing with "God bless Mama, Daddy, Busia, Dziadzia, and everybody," and jump back into bed.

This was the prayer I repeated every night. Busia and Dziadzia were the names children called their grandparents in Poland, where my grandmother and grandfather were born. After Dziadzia died, Busia said it was important to pray for him. I barely remembered Daddy, but I prayed for him anyway. Every night I remembered a particular prayer my mother taught me before she left me with Busia:

> *Now I lay me down to sleep.*
> *I pray the Lord my soul to keep.*
> *If I should die before I wake,*
> *I pray the Lord my soul to take.*

Busia emerges from her bedroom to tuck me in. The glow from the stove lights her way to my bedside and casts the shadow of her small body twelve feet high onto the wall and ceiling.

"It so cold," Busia says. "God bless you. See you in morning. Tomorrow is be good day." She plants a thin-lipped dry kiss on my cheek, returns to her bedroom, and switches off the light. "Everything is good," I hear her mutter. "*Dzięki Bogu*, thanks God, very fine, very nice, very good, very sweet."

I can hear the wind howling and beating against the house. The walls creak and struggle to stand against this preview of the coming winter—a winter that holds in its cold hands more threats than the harrowing walk to the coal bin.

I remember waking up one cold morning in late November to Busia hurrying past my bed carrying kindling wood. While I pretend not to wake up, Busia pushes paper and dry sticks into the stove. The few coals that lived through the night ignite and the kindling flares up. Then she shoves a big log through the open door of the stove, twisting and jerking it until it slides in and crashes into the fire. She uses the small shovel to remove the ashes and clinkers, coal's incombustible residue, which has fallen to the bottom of the stove during the night. The house would soon be warm.

"Time get up, Lenuś," Busia calls from the kitchen where she is already building another fire in the cooking stove.

Teeth chattering, I crawl out of bed, shivering and covered with goose bumps while I jump into my clothes and hurry to the kitchen sink. As I move the pump handle up and down, water rises from the well near the house and spills icy cold onto my hands and face.

"Most everybody farm have it hot and running water," Busia says apologetically. Our farm, however, had changed little since it was built in the 1870s "But we got it 'lectric," she adds, to atone, just in case God thinks she is complaining.

After I dry my hands and face, I put on my coat and boots and head for the outhouse. I return flapping my arms to warm up.

Breakfast is a bowl of oatmeal with brown sugar, butter, and milk. Afterwards, I run out to the mailbox where the first Christmas cards of the season have been delivered by the U.S. Postal Service. We sit down at the kitchen table and Busia opens them one at a time. The early cards are from England and Poland, in colored envelopes made of tissue paper and stamped with pictures of mustachioed men. Each card contains a note in Polish, parts of which Busia reads aloud. I tape these messages from the outside world to the dining room wall.

Busia opens one last envelope and reads the letter silently. When she finishes, she folds it and puts it back into the envelope, slipping it into her apron pocket.

I fiddle with the envelopes on the kitchen table until Busia emerges from her bedroom, having filed the mysterious letter in her cedar box. She is cheery and smiling, and whatever it was that distracted her appears to have passed. She has decided it is time to begin addressing our own Christmas cards.

"We send it all overseas cards tomorrow," she explains. We examine each card and admire the pictures of Jesus, Mary, Joseph, and assorted angels and shepherds. Busia reads each verse aloud.

"This one go to *ciocia*," she announces, setting aside the Three Kings for her aunt in Detroit, "and this one to Franciszek," she says of an angel floating above a sprig of holly that is destined for her brother in Poland. She meticulously addresses each envelope, then writes a few words in every card and signs it, indicating her relationship to the addressee, adding "*i rodziny*," and family. As she finishes each card, she hands it to me, and I slide it into an envelope, lick the glue on its flap, and seal it. The week before, Busia had left an envelope of money in the mailbox with the flag up, and in its place the mailman left five-cent postage stamps. I carefully tear one stamp from the sheet for each envelope, lick it, and affix it. Then I stack the cards in a neat pile. The glue is delicious.

When the last card is stamped, Busia sighs and proclaims, "Now, we make it coffee cake. It be fun, no?" She flexes her arthritic hands and tugs at each gnarled knuckle.

After pulling spoons and measuring cups out of the cupboard, Busia begins by melting two cakes of yeast in warm water. Over the stove she melts butter and sugar in a pan, dumps it into a large mixing bowl, adds eggs, milk, and vanilla, then flour and then yeast. She sits in a kitchen chair, rests the bowl in her lap, and beats the gooey batter as hard as she can, fighting with the sticky dough, her upper arm jiggling as she wields the spoon and folds in the raisins. Busia laughs and sings in Polish, "*Czerwone Jabłuszko*," explaining that she once was a young farm girl in Poland, like the girl in the song, tending ducks and geese by the lake near her house.

When the dough is beaten, Busia puts it on a shelf above the stove and covers it with a cloth. Now, we will wait two hours while the dough grows to twice its size. The radio blares "How Much Is That Doggie in the Window?"

Both of us jump when we hear someone climbing the creaky back steps. Busia drops her wooden spoon, turns off the radio, and creeps to the window.

When she opens the door, the landlord enters the kitchen, leading a man and a woman. The tall, red-faced man is wearing overalls and a denim barn jacket. The stout, serious-looking woman is dressed in a flowered skirt and a baggy waist-length jacket, her hands stuffed into its pockets. Her forehead is furrowed with four deep, pink wrinkles.

"These people I write you about. I bring see house," the landlord says politely, adjusting the chewing tobacco in his mouth.

"Hope you don't mind us barging in like this, Mrs.," the woman volunteers flatly, with a forced smile.

"I no think you come today," Busia replies, wiping flour on her apron and leaving sprinkles of white all over the sleeve of her red sweater.

I twist a piece of coffee cake dough off the wooden spoon with my fingers and pop it into my mouth as the three visitors disappear into the dining room.

Burying my head in Busia's apron, I ask what the people want and she tells me "*Cicho*," cautioning with her finger to her lips. In silence, I stand by the coffee cake, as the intruders shuffle through the house. Busia takes the bowl down from the shelf and gives the rising dough three heavy whacks. Then she sits down in the dining room to work on her rug, me beside her. Silently she hooks the rag strips into circles, three and four long strips, before the heavy boots descend from the second floor. The woman says, "If I had my druthers, I'd make one o' these into a sewing room." I wondered what druthers were and why she needed them to sew.

A gust of cold air blows into the dining room as the intruders reappear. The landlord ushers them into Busia's bedroom while she rips the thread off the last strip of cloth she has sewn to the rug.

9

The landlord pulls back the curtains and blankets that close off the frozen living room and parlor. The intruders peer in, like people at the Armada Fair peering into the rabbit coops.

"Thank you, Mrs.," the landlord says, shifting his weight from foot to foot. The man and woman nod.

When the strangers leave, Busia sits quietly in her rocker for a long time. Then she tunes the radio to WJLB's Polish-language program. I watch as the rings of color grow around Busia's new rug. While the radio announcer is praising Alka-Seltzer, Busia explains that I was born in Michigan and she was born in Poland.

"*Oy yoy yoy*," Busia says, her favorite phrase of surprise. "I born in a Poland. I come to America 1913 very young girl. I come on big boat. Such a big boat, have three chimney. Uncle Stasiu live in Hamtramck. He say me and my sister America is rich. Everybody rich in America. Street in America is gold, he say," Busia laughs, revealing an eyetooth, one of the few remaining teeth in her mouth. She lifts her hand to cover her smile.

"My mother have nine children, so my sister we go. We go to America. For two weeks we ride on a boat. We eat herring and bread. We have storm. At night boat rock this way, that way." She tilts her head from left to right imitating the ocean waves. "People get sick but I no. We pray. Then we come to New York and on big train to Michigan."

I ask her what the intruders wanted. Busia hesitates. "No forget, Lenuś, I no own this property." When she speaks, she cannot pronounce "th" because there is no "th" in Polish, and so "this, that, these, them, those, and the" become "dis, dat, dese, dem, doze, and da"; "think and thank" become "tink and tank."

Meanwhile, the yeasty dough on the shelf has risen to twice its original size. Busia puts the dough in two loaf pans and covers them with dish towels. Then she takes *pierogi* stuffed with potato and cheese out of the icebox and boils them for lunch. When she made them,

I could not say. Busia was always cooking, always boiling a piece of beef, a head of cabbage, potatoes. My mother and I later called this standard concoction "beef oosheekooshee" because when we asked what was for dinner, Busia would say in her Polish-English mix, "*Ja beef uszykuję,*" I am preparing beef.

After lunch, Busia removes the cakes from the shelf, sprinkles a mixture of brown sugar, butter, and cinnamon (which she called "see NAH moon") on top, and slides them into the oven. She reaches into the woodbox for more kindling, knowing just how much wood the stove needs to make the oven right for coffee cake. Then I get the best treat of all: to lick the topping bowl.

When the coffee cakes are done Busia takes them out of the oven and places them on a breadboard. We return to cutting rag strips for the rug. Busia talks about the old country. Her grandmother, she says, told her that as a little girl the family lived in a dugout house and at night could hear wolves scratch at the door above them.

When the cakes are cool, Busia slices a piece for each of us and slathers them with butter.

The coffee cake is warm and delicious. The baking of the *babka* is a ritual that took place every week that we lived in the old farmhouse.

The next day, I go outside early to put the Christmas cards in the mailbox. I raise the little red flag on the side so the mailman will know there is something in the box to be picked up. Although it is still November, most of the cards have a long way to travel before they reach relatives in the old country. I cannot stop thinking about Christmas, especially when Auntie Mary comes over to help Busia wrap a package in brown paper and mail old clothes to Poland.

On weekends some of Busia's children always came to visit and they brought my cousins. There were twelve aunts and uncles—my mother's four brothers and two sisters and their spouses. After being smothered with kisses and hugs, Busia loved to wait on them and bring out food while they talked to one another.

This weekend, Busia's twin sons, John and Joe, and their wives, Helen and Louise, are seated around a card table in the kitchen playing pinochle. They laugh and chatter about what everyone in the family is doing. They eat pieces of Busia's coffee cake and recall their lives as children on the farms their family had worked, three farms in a row on 32 Mile Road. They called them Pickwick Place, the Sullivan Farm, and the Foote Farm, all named for the people who owned them when they were built. Uncle Joe and Auntie Louise own the Sullivan Farm, the neighboring farm to the west. At their house, I saw my first television and later watched *The Mickey Mouse Club*.

Uncle John and Auntie Helen are my godparents. They have two daughters, Cynthia and Cathy, and will eventually have two more daughters and a son. Auntie Louise will have a son in eight years and die of an indeterminate thrombosis soon after. Her son will not remember her; her daughters, Sandra and Christine, will be traumatized. Uncle Joe will remarry and inherit two sons from his new wife, and they will have a daughter together.

Busia is by the stove making coffee in her scratched and stained old pot. Someone says, "Say Ma, you got any popcorn?"

I watch from the dining room where I am building a town on the floor for my cousins to see, the same town I build over and over out of a small box of toy cars, Lego bricks, and Lincoln Logs. We are all listening to find out if there is to be popcorn.

"Maybe some in field need pick it," Busia says, and before anyone can tell her not to bother, she has on her coat, gloves, boots, and babushka.

"Can we go?" I call from the dining room.

"You come," Busia answers. I am ready in an instant, and the four girls trail close behind.

The moon is glowing and looks like the piece of cheese I'm told it is made of. It is a crisp, shadowy November night. We walk from the porch to the barn and then down the lane to Busia's little garden, where some hardy stalks of popcorn still stand.

I spot one ear of corn. Busia finds four. We pull off the crackly husks. These are the second crop of ears, runts that didn't have time or strength for a full season's growth. But if we are lucky, they will pop just the same.

"Good," Busia announces, "We finish."

We walk back to the house with the corn, talking about how good it will taste and about the moonlight and the way it lights up the land, five cousins trailing Busia like ducklings.

When we get back inside, the aunts and uncles are conferring in hushed tones that turn quickly into exaggerated cheers for the popcorn we have found.

We proud pickers shell our treasure, and soon it is popping loudly over the stove as Busia shakes the kettle until she almost loses her balance. "Those little buggers will still pop, eh little squirts?" says Uncle John, smiling a crooked smile at us kids. Salted and buttered, the popcorn is delicious.

Busia spends the rest of the evening making sure everyone has enough to eat and drink. Her boys and their wives talk until nine o'clock. I watch and listen to the mix of Polish and English that fills the house until the cousins fall asleep and I grow tired and wander to my bed behind the dining room stove.

On Monday morning, I awaken to discover that snow has fallen during the night, and so I jump up and run from window to window. Busia advises me to bundle up before I go outside; I stuff myself into my snow pants that are at least a size too small.

The snow has floated down and settled in a fluffy layer over the trees, the bushes, and the buildings. Everything is covered with a clean, white blanket. I dash from bush to bush, shaking each one, watching the branches magically appear as the snow falls to the ground. Some of the icicles hanging from the shed are so long I can reach them, so I snap one off, taking time to examine the way dripping water has been trapped on its journey to the ground. Then I lick it before smashing it.

The back door opens and Busia emerges, bundled up and carrying the empty coal pail. She remarks about the cold in Polish, "*Zimno!*"

And when I repeat it, she laughs, then disappears into the coal bin, reappearing minutes later lugging a pail full of coal. She sets it on the porch, goes into the garage, and comes out with a large log from Uncle Hank's woods.

We spend the rest of the day indoors. The coal pail is full and so is the woodbox. Busia is in her bedroom rearranging the contents of her dresser.

"I'm going upstairs," I call to her.

"It so cold," she advises, "put on flannel shirt." When I open the upstairs door, a gust of cold air rushes at me, but I am warmly dressed and I like the exhilarating shivers that come over me as I stare up into the huge second floor.

"Close it door," Busia calls, "You born in a barn?"

Upstairs is like another house—five rooms of stored and unused things from other days, all for me, I thought. Some of the things belonged to Busia, some of them were left behind by the Foote family, who lived there before us.

I love the big old radio, which is as tall as me and stands on four carved legs. I try to turn it on, but it does not work. There is a heavy brown bed made of swirled iron. There are clothes racks where Busia sometimes dries the wash. There are rolls of wallpaper in the same patterns as the paper on the walls. I don my grandfather's old tweed hat and bounce on the old bedsprings. I look at pictures on the walls and stare at a strange glass box containing a crucifix with a snake crawling on a skull beneath it.

I had noticed the door to the attic before, but something always prevented me from opening it. The attic was above the one-story section of the farmhouse, over the chilly parlor.

I imagine that no one has been in the attic for a long time, as I step cautiously to the door and undo the latch and push. The door creaks and scrapes, then springs open and slams against the wall behind it.

A musty smell hits my face, and the sight of the dusty gray attic makes me gasp; there are so many things in it! It is full! I run over to a stack of enormous picture frames, some of wood and some painted gold. There are at least three different beds in the attic, the parts leaning here and there next to jugs and jars and vases of all kinds. There are magazines, old and yellowed, with pictures of people wearing odd clothes. They look strange, especially the women's mouths and hair and their tiny pinched waists.

At the far end of the attic is a window. I had looked at the small panes of glass from the outside before, but now I can step up and look down to the yard and straight ahead at the high branches of the trees. I can see far across the field to Uncle Joe's farm.

I turn back to the attic and walk along the center of the floor. Where the roof slants down, there are no floor boards, and I can see the strips of board with plaster oozing between them—the ceiling of the closed-off parlor below.

I find a copper chandelier, which I drag out of the attic and vow to polish, and I pull out an odd-looking carpet sweeper, which I try pushing across the wall-to-wall rag rugs left behind by the Foote family. I work my way through piles of things abandoned by people I do not know. I find a lantern with a wire handle, baskets of many shapes and sizes, a table, a wooden rake with two missing teeth, books, and a wooden weaving contraption that must have been used to make the rag rugs.

Then I discover a stack of phonograph records and an old Victrola just like the one we play with at Uncle Joe's house. I crank it up, no electricity required, and play the records one after the other. They are all very strange and scratchy. I have never heard anything quite like them on the radio. I pick one by Paul Whiteman and His Orchestra as my favorite:

Whispering while you cuddle near me,
Whispering so no one can hear me,
Each little whisper seems to cheer me.
I know it's true, there's no one, dear, but you....

The voice on the record is accompanied by whining, whistling instruments. It is a happy song, and I play it over and over.

Downstairs, I can hear Busia talking and a man's voice answering. The back door closes, an engine starts. I run to the tiny window above the side porch and see the landlord pulling away in his old red pickup.

I bathed in a round metal tub behind the kitchen stove. Busia filled the tub with water she heated a kettleful at a time on the wood stove. She hung a curtain on a clothesline around the tub. The warm stove on one side and the kitchen wall on the other formed a cozy private room.

The farmhouse had no bathroom, though most of the other houses on 32 Mile Road did. Heating kettles of water was a lot of trouble, but I had my bath every Saturday, no matter what. Once in a while, I could hear my grandmother fixing bath water for herself after I went to bed, but most of the time I never knew when she bathed or took what she called a sponge bath, just that she always smelled clean and good when I rocked next to her in her rocking chair.

Sunday morning means church. I hurry to get ready. Then Busia and I wait at the kitchen window for Uncle Hank to pick us up. Busia moves from room to room checking. Are all the lights off? Are the stoves both set to burn until we return? She pumps herself a glass of ice cold water. Then she pops peppermint candies into her purse to offer during the ride home. Busia is wearing her designated church dress—a shiny floral print with rhinestone buttons—and her best coat, which is a little too big for her. She dons her navy blue straw hat with big nylon flowers all along the rim and fusses with wisps of her hair, which she always wears pulled into a neat little bun at the back of her head.

Finally, at ten minutes to ten, Uncle Hank's Buick appears in the driveway. We rush outside and climb in. We will surely be late today. Busia sits in the front seat, and I am in the back. In years to come, Uncle Hank and Auntie Betty will have five rambunctious girls who will climb all over me and chatter in my teenage face in the car. But these early rides to church are the business of a mother and her dutiful son.

Because the Mass has already begun, people look up from their missals disapprovingly as Busia and I parade to the only empty pew, which, as always, is at the front of the church. Uncle Hank is an usher so he gets to stay in the back. Grossly unfair, it seems to me. The priest chants in Latin, and the choir, with its one powerful female voice and trail of childish voices, responds on cue.

Once we make it to a seat, I feel safe once Mass has begun. After we sit down, people stop staring at us and we begin being part of the crowd. Busia takes out her rosary. Her lips move as she repeats prayers to herself in Polish. No one else is Polish—except for Mrs. Pavlik, who sometimes chats with Busia as we exit. She is Uncle Harry's mother and smiles a lot and also wears a hat decorated with fake flowers.

I watch the priest and the altar boys and follow along in my missalette. The pictures in the book show what the priest is doing, and here and there I can read words my mother taught me.

It is very important to do the right thing at the right time in church. A woman across the aisle begins to stand when everyone else is beginning to kneel. It is the most embarrassing thing that can happen.

Sometimes, when the priest varies even the smallest detail, half of the congregants do one thing and the other half do another. Neither side gives in, so it is difficult to know what to do. The quandary is less embarrassing when everyone is mixed up than when it happens to one person all alone, like the woman standing when she is supposed to be kneeling. She slides sheepishly into a kneeling position, as if she had meant to kneel all along.

Busia never stops praying her rosary and seems oblivious to the woman's transgression. I try hard to pray and not watch the people who are mostly watching each other. But when Mass is finally over, I am glad to be part of the small group that sneaks to the side door instead of funneling through the main exit and shaking hands with the priest. Busia says, "Maybe we not should use this door." But she does it anyway.

Uncle Hank visits with his mother for an hour after church, and Busia makes coffee in her percolator and brings out milk and a coffee cake. Uncle Hank instructs me in how to take care of things in the cold weather. I understand that this is their special time together, and I go upstairs or outside and busy myself and ask no questions.

After Uncle Hank went home to finish his chores, someone else often came to visit on Sunday. Busia's other three sons have children of their own, my cousins, and as often as not there is another cousin "on the way." Eventually, Busia will have twenty-three grandchildren. On Sunday afternoons for many years to come, we played Hide-the-Button or Drop-the-Clothespin, or Mother-May-I. The kitchen in the old farmhouse was perfect for Mother-May-I: a very long room, so giant steps and baby steps could continue for a long time until someone made it all the way to "mother." When the weather was nice, we went outside. Sometimes we played Hide-and-Seek in the big yard. But most of the time we headed for the barn.

There was always something to do in the barn. There were the old granary bins, like a maze of rooms in a big empty house. There were bales of hay to jump on, and there was the rope swing.

On this particular Sunday in early December, Uncle John and Auntie Helen are visiting with Cynthia, who is a year younger than I but already in school, and Cathy, who is a toddler. We are on our way to play in the barn. Cynthia runs ahead. "I'll beat you guys to the rope," she hollers back.

I run after her, and Cathy lags behind. When we reach the barn, Cynthia is already inside and climbing on the wooden ledge between the haymow and the center of the barn.

When the barn was used years ago, the tractor would pull the wagon into the center of the barn where it was next to the haymow, and the bales could be unloaded and stacked there. Wagons of grain were unloaded into the bins on the other side.

Cynthia grabs the rope suspended from the very top of the barn and hanging loose near the built-in ladder that leads to the ceiling. Standing on the divider, which was short enough to climb yet sturdy enough for grown men to walk on and to support the bales of hay, she clings to the rope and gives herself a push with her feet. "Woo-hoo," she screams, swinging free at least two feet above the barn floor. Out and back she swings until she brings herself to a stop on the ledge. "You wanna do it, Lennie?" she calls.

I have done this many times before, but it never seems to lose its thrill. Climbing onto the ledge, I grab the rope and shove myself as hard as I can. We play on the rope for a long time, taking turns and swinging together. Cathy stands by the ladder and watches. She only says "uh-uh" when we ask her if she wants to try it and starts turning somersaults in the hay and rolling down the stacks of bales.

Whenever I got a bright idea, I would say, "I know!" and my cousins would listen. Now, standing on the other side of the divider outside the haymow, I call out, "I know! I can climb up on top of the granary bins!"

While Cynthia stands by the rope and watches, I climb up the built-in ladder to the empty loft above the bins and look around. There are still traces of straw on the floor. I step to the edge and look down at her and Cathy.

"Ooo, you're so high," she says. I am at least six feet above the barn floor.

"Now hand me the rope," I order. Cynthia brings the rope over and climbs high enough on the ladder to hand it to me. Then she descends and stands across the center of the barn in the haymow to watch my performance.

I hold tight to the rope and stare down at the old floorboards, worn and broken by the wheels of countless wagons and tractors. I am not sure if I can swing all the way to the divider and I do not know where I will be when the rope stops swinging, but I call down, "Should I jump?"

"I don't know," Cynthia says, shrugging her shoulders, staring up at me wide-eyed, and prepared for the consequences—like the nurse she would eventually become.

I squeeze the rope until my knuckles turn white. Then I wait for what seems like forever. Cynthia just stares at me. Cathy stops playing in the hay and looks up.

At that moment, I hold on to the rope and jump off the ledge, soaring across the barn, swinging out over the divider, and sailing back to the bins. I kick the wall and shove myself back to the divider, flying back and forth at least five feet above the barn floor. Just when I am not sure I can hold on any longer, the rope slows down, and I slide to the floor, landing in hay inches away from a pitchfork, its prongs pointing straight up.

My cousins run over to me laughing, "Wow! That looks like fun. Wow! You were so high!" My heart is beating hard. "Do you want to try it?"

"Move the pitchfork!" Cynthia commands.

Just then we hear voices from the house and it is time for Cynthia and Cathy to go home. Afternoons in the barn passed quickly.

Autumn is almost gone now and winter is grabbing hold. The time before Christmas passes slowly, and I watch every day for signs of the coming holiday—the music on the radio, snowfall, and Busia's preparations.

"What do you want for Christmas?" I ask Cynthia as we run through the muddy driveway. But she has already reached the house and is bragging about what we have done as she opens the back door. Cathy nods and says "yah" after everything her sister says.

Uncle John says we should be careful so we don't crack our heads open. Auntie Helen tells us listen to Uncle John because he knows what he is talking about. And Busia stands by the sink muttering, "*Oy yoy yoy*."

Winter

Every day, I ask Busia when are we going to get our Christmas tree, and every day she tells me it is too early. "Go see maybe mailman bring Christmas cards," she diverts, knowing that Christmas really begins when cards from far away start arriving in the mailbox at the end of our long gravel driveway.

One day in mid-December, Busia is boiling oatmeal for breakfast as usual when she turns to me and says, "Today we go get it Christmas tree." When she says "Christmas" it sounds like "Crease Moose."

I am so eager that I can hardly gulp down my breakfast.

Afterwards, Busia puts on her furry winter coat, her boots with the fake fur around the tops, and her wool gloves with the pearl flowers and tucks her hair under her black babushka.

"We dress up warm," she says, "cold outside today. I think is maybe snow." When she says "think" it sounds like "tink." She makes sure that my boots are buckled and hands me a scarf.

Before we leave the house, Busia checks all the stoves and gets a drink of water and a peppermint candy for each of us; then she makes the sign of the cross and we go outside.

"Brrr, *zimno!*" Busia exclaims, stomping her boots in the snow and deciding whether we should take the sled or the wagon. "Oh, I think is enough snow we can take it sled," she concludes.

I run to the garage and pull out the old sled I found in the barn. It looks as though it has seen many winters, but it is still in pretty good shape even though much of the paint is chipped off. There is just enough snow on the ground for the sled to slide, and the air is just cold enough to keep the snow from melting.

Busia is on the other side of the garage rummaging through the shelves that Dziadzia built along one wall to hold tools and his cigar boxes loaded with nails and screws. Just the right things always seemed to be there when they were needed. Busia finds a saw and a ball of cord, which she places securely on the sled.

"Okay, we ready go!" she announces.

We walk down the lane past the barn all the way to the creek. Busia calls, "Slow down! I no can walk so fast!"

When we reach the creek, we stop for a moment to watch the icy water moving swiftly past the snowy banks. On the other side of the creek by the lane to the woods stands a row of Christmas trees.

"There they are!" I holler and run ahead pulling the sled so fast the saw and cord fall off. Busia picks them up and follows me to the trees.

Eight pine trees of various shapes and sizes have grown at the edge of the farm, where Dziadzia planted them years ago.

"Which one should we cut?" I ask and offer advice. "This one is really nice! Let's get this one! It's so big!" It is a beautiful bushy tree with short needles.

"*Oy yoy yoy*," Busia studies the tree and decides, "We take big one; if we no take now be too big for Crease Moose tree next year."

She hands me the saw and I start sawing. It is much harder than I imagine to cut through the small trunk, especially on my knees with the bottom branches slapping me in the face, but Busia assures me that I can do it, and with a swoosh the tree falls to the ground.

As we are tying the tree to the sled, huge fluffy flakes of snow start to fall. The two of us begin the long walk home. It snows harder and harder, straight down, gently, until the sky is a mass of white swirls, streaks, and spots.

"Is good thing winter," Busia proclaims.

"Why?" I ask.

"Because if no be winter, we be walk in a rain," she laughs.

I laugh too and catch snowflakes on my tongue. We are both pulling the sled now, and the snow is sticking to our clothes as we walk back home. Busia says we have Dziadzia to thank for our Christmas tree.

"Is Crease Moose time," Busia says, "Nothing can spoil it Crease Moose." She looks down at me. "Everything is all right. Is beautiful outside. We not should worry!" She twirls herself around almost falling over. Then she grabs my hand and we spin around together. "*Oy yoy yoy*," she exclaims, patting her chest.

"Merry Crease Moose!" she sings, "*Wesołych Świąt! Bożego Narodzenia! W żłobie leży któż pobieżny....*" Busia's words drift across the silent windless lane.

When we get back to the house, I shake the snow off the tree on the porch, then I drag it inside by the stem. Busia takes down the curtains and blankets that hang between the living room and dining room. Through the holidays, they will remain down. The tree will stand in a window that can be seen from the road. This will also make more room in the house for the big family gathering on Christmas Day. It also means that more wood and coal must be brought inside every day.

The cold air rushes into the dining room, but Busia puts a chunk of wood in each stove. The fire will soon warm the frozen living room. We move a table out of the spot where the Christmas tree should stand. There is one corner of the room with a window on each of the adjoining walls, and the lights of the tree will be seen outdoors from both windows.

Busia rushes around moving furniture, dusting, and telling me where to put things. When the living room is ready, we open the door to the cold upstairs and bring down a big cardboard box that contains all the decorations.

First, Busia holds the tree upright while I secure it in the stand. We place it in the corner, with its best side facing the room. The radio is playing Christmas music in the dining room, and I insist on turning it up louder. I rush so much to get the decorations out of the box that I start running rings around Busia. "Take it time!" she urges, but I do not.

The strings of lightbulbs are tangled together. I hold the pile while Busia unwinds them and places them carefully on the tree. At the bottom she attaches the string of bubblers—weird lights shaped like cupcakes with candles in them. After they are plugged in for a few minutes, bubbles begin to run up and down the long candle-shaped portion of the bulb.

Busia carefully unpacks her two most precious glass ornaments and hands one to me, ornaments my mother bought before I was born. We hang the shiny colored balls on the tree and the little stars and bells and angels and Santas, one by one until the tree is full. Busia goes into the kitchen and brings out a box of peppermint candy canes she ordered from the bakery man. We hang them on the tree. Then she climbs onto a kitchen chair, her hand on my shoulder, and places the star at the treetop. "Hold it chair so no move," she instructs.

When the decorations are all hung, we head back into the kitchen where Busia begins popping the popcorn that she has stashed away for this special purpose. She tells me to put a long piece of thread in a needle. I thread two pieces: one for myself and one for Busia. I can smell the popcorn as it bursts against the lid of the old metal pan.

When she has popped four big bowls of *kukurydza*, Busia sits down in the dining room near the stove, in view of the Christmas tree. There we string the white kernels all the rest of the afternoon, Busia rocking in her chair deftly manipulating her needle, hardly ever breaking a kernel, me, jumping up and down, so amazing is her ability. "Is American style," she says. "In Poland corn is for cows."

By the time evening comes, all the strings of popcorn are on the tree, and it is covered with dripping, sparkling tinsel we have placed strand by strand, as my mother taught me, on each branch. We have turned the Christmas tree lights on and all the house lights off. The finished tree is a splendid pyramid shining with colored lights and ornaments.

Busia gives me a quick hug and says, "No is beautiful?"

We sit and admire the tree for a long time before we say "*Dobranoc,*" good night, and go to bed.

Auntie Helen comes on Saturday morning to take Busia to town. I have saved ten quarters and some pennies from the money that my uncles

gave me when they came to visit. I don't know what it will be, but on this trip to town I intend to buy Busia a Christmas present, and I am going to pick it out myself.

"Now, we're going to a few other places first," Auntie Helen says when Busia isn't listening, "and then I'll take Grandma to the car and you pick something out in the dime store." What a treat it is to go shopping in Armada.

At the grocery store Busia buys flour, sugar, and other things the bakery man and milkman do not bring during the week. Then we go to the mill and buy flour sack prints for making dresses and aprons and dish towels. We go to the drugstore, and finally to the dime store.

The dime store is the best store of all. I hurry up and down the creaky floorboard aisles looking at all the things for sale. There are stacks and bins of toys—little cars and trucks and trains. There is a whole aisle filled with kitchen utensils: cake pans, rolling pins, brooms. But Busia already has all those things, so I go to the cosmetics aisle and find a big rack of perfume bottles with a sign above it: $1. I choose a bottle decorated with lilies of the valley, like the ones that grow in our yard around the front porch.

I have to be careful so Busia does not see me carrying the perfume. I sneak into the aisle where the ladies' clothing is stacked in neat little bins and stand on tiptoe to examine some aprons and dresses and scarves. I find a pile of long flannel nightgowns next to a sign: $1.25. Just then, Auntie Helen peeks around the corner.

"How ya doin'?" she asks conspiratorially, almost in a whisper.

"Do I have enough to buy these two things?" I want to know.

She tells me I will have 26 cents left after I pay for the perfume and the nightgown.

"I'm gonna take Grandma out to the car now," Auntie Helen says. "You stay here till you see us go, and then you pay for your things." On her way out, she says something to the clerk at the cash register. I ponder my purchases and the head back to the toy aisle and pick out a tiny red metal car with a 25¢ sticker on it. I wait until I see Busia and Auntie Helen leave. Then I take my three items up to the counter, pay the lady, tell her thank you, and carry my bag out to the car waiting for me in front of the store.

"Look what I bought," I announce as I get in the back seat, pulling my car out of the bag.

"Oh, that's nice!" Auntie Helen says cheerfully, covering for me.

"Very good," says Busia coyly, "Is all you buy?"

I reply with an evasive "What?"

"I no chew my cabbage twice," Busia says, and Auntie Helen laughs.

I don't know exactly what that is supposed to mean, except that when Busia says it, she is finished talking. When we get home from our shopping spree and are pulling into the driveway, we see the Ford pickup parked near the corn crib. The landlord is pointing toward the creek and raising his chin as he talks to a man wearing a furry cap and holding his arms crossed over his chest.

"*Jezus Maria*," Busia sighs and throws her hands into the air. I peek over the seat and demand to know what he is doing at the house again, looking back and forth from Busia to my aunt. The man in the furry cap points at the house. Then the landlord spots our car. The men jump into the landlord's truck and wave at us as they pass in the driveway. Busia looks out the opposite window. "Look at birds in tree," she says, pointing.

When we are in the house, I hide the Christmas presents under my bed. After sandwiches, Busia talks with Auntie Helen while I bring out all my toys to see how well the new car fits into my town on the floor.

That evening, Auntie Helen spoke Polish and kept asking questions about the landlord, but Busia just kept saying that she couldn't understand his English. That was the first time Busia ever made sandwiches, which Auntie Helen told her were so easy to make. Busia was skeptical. "Cold sanveech is no good like hot soup," she said, but she began making them anyway and calling them *kanapki*.

Every day before Christmas is a busy day. One day Busia makes cookies. I help her cut the rolled dough into Santas and trees and stars. Some of the cookies have holes in them so they can be tied with ribbons and hung on the tree. We make so many she has to go into the pantry and find extra containers for them.

On another day Busia makes candy out of butter and sugar, melting them in a pot on the wood stove and scooping the batter into a flat pan. When it cools, she cuts it into squares. I crack walnuts for her to scatter across the top, gently so the shells do not shatter. Then I glue the two shell halves back together, with a string sticking out of the top end. When I finish, I take all the glued nut shells and with Busia's help dip them into melted wax colored with crayon. Busia lets me stand on a chair and hang the little ornaments high on the Christmas tree.

Finally, the biggest workday of all arrives: Christmas Eve. The fire in the kitchen stove blazes as Busia sits by the table rolling stuffed cabbages. She puts a huge ham in the oven. She begins working on a coffee cake and rolls *gołąbki* well into the afternoon, scooping rice and ground meat into cabbage leaves. All day we work, cooking food for Christmas. Busia says these are the same foods her mother and grandmother prepared for the holiday in Poland. By evening, both of us are ready for a nap before it is time for Midnight Mass.

Uncle Hank comes alone and early. Auntie Betty never comes because she is not Catholic. My mother said theirs is "a mixed marriage," the same transgression for which Uncle Joe was disowned by Dziadzia, who had already died when Hank married Betty at the side altar, where mixed marriages were performed. We are ready, refreshed from our nap, Busia wearing her finest floral print dress.

The church is crowded, but for me Midnight Mass is the best time. Lighted trees illuminate the altar and a crèche fills the side altar where Uncle Hank and Auntie Betty got married. It is the one time in church when we do not have to traipse to the last remaining pews at the front. Tonight, there will be standing room only, and we are already comfortably settled mid-church.

Before long, the choir begins to sing. It is bigger than usual, with extra adult male voices that sing out with gusto. I do not dare turn and stare into the choir loft to see who they are. It is customary to wait until after Mass and stare up at the choir loft on the way out of church.

I know all the words to "Silent Night," "O Come All Ye Faithful," "The First Noel," and "Hark! The Herald Angels Sing," and I wish I could be up in the choir too. They sing the carols so enthusiastically that every-one in the church is alert, even the few children who have been permitted to come. Uncle Hank gives me a nickel for every carol I memorize.

When we get home from church, Busia makes ham sandwiches with bread from the bakery man. She and Uncle Hank have lots of *chrzan* on theirs, extra hot horseradish. I opt for butter after plugging in the tree lights for Uncle Hank to see. Beneath the tree lie four presents, two of which I have wrapped myself and tied with red ribbon, as my mother taught me.

"Who are the presents for?" Uncle Hanks asks.

"These two are for Busia," I point to the ones I have wrapped.

"And two for somebody else," Busia laughs.

Uncle Hank soon leaves for home, and I am growing so impatient that I beg Busia to open her presents.

"I want you to open them now, please Busia," my favorite word, "please."

"Okay, we open now. Bring here."

I lead Busia into the living room. "You sit down on the davenport," I order and run to get the presents from under the tree.

"Open this one first," I command, handing her the smaller package.

"What this?" Busia says, laughing shyly, as though she doesn't de-serve the present, and adjusting a loose wisp of hair. She undoes the ribbon and wrapping slowly.

"*Oy yoy oy*! Pear-foon!" she exclaims. "I gonna smell it good now." She dabs a bit of the perfume awkwardly on her neck, near her ears, as if no one had ever given her perfume.

I push the large package into her hands. "Open this now," I insist.

Busia unwraps the second gift faster. "*Oy yoy oy*!" she says, "I need it nightgown very much." She unfolds it and lifts it out of the box, admiring the pale blue dotted with tiny blue flowers. Busia gently touches the white lace around the collar. "Very nice, very good, thank you very much," she says, and gives me a hug and a kiss. "Okay, we go to bed now. Is two clock already."

"Do we have to go to bed right now?" I stall.

Busia laughs. "Oh, I almost forget!" She steps over to the tree, leans down to pick up the two remaining presents, and hands them to me. "Merry Crease Moose!"

I cannot hold back. The first box contains a pair of mittens Busia had knitted for me when I wasn't looking. It also holds two pairs of socks and some underwear. The second box is very large, and I am not even careful not to rip the poinsettia paper to shreds. When I open the box, there is a miniature gas station inside. It has two pumps with little hoses and numbers in the windows that really turn when you put the pretend gas into the cars and trucks. Inside the gas station are two wreckers and two little cars.

"Oh, Busia! This is great! It fits right in with my town." After hugs and kisses, I go back to my gift.

Busia retreats into her bedroom and puts on her new nightgown. When she comes out, I am still examining the gas station. "You like?" she asks.

"I love it," I answer, without looking up. Then I see Busia in her new nightgown. "Oh, yes, it looks very good. You look pretty." And she does, with her gray hair in a bun, her gold-rimmed glasses, her smile with missing teeth, and her "*nos jak cebula*," as she often said, "nose like an onion. She looks very beautiful and very tired. We stare at the tree one more time before we unplug it. The big day is ahead of us.

As I finally get into my bed behind the stove, I hear Busia's silence as she says her prayers, and then I hear her say, "Good night, Merry Crease Moose. And don't worry nothing."

As she says this, with a sigh, I believe her, believe we will never have to leave the farm. I stare at the shadowy ceiling. The fire crackles and spits in the stove beside me. There is nothing more anyone could want to do on a day like today, only to fall asleep knowing there is another day ahead.

The morning is quiet—Busia and I sweep snow off the porch, fill the woodbox and set eight big logs behind the stove, getting food ready for the table. There is plenty of wood to last all day and through the night. Every day we save electricity, but now the tree can be lit all Christmas day, and I plug in the lights as soon as I wake up. Outside, the day is perfect; the snow is fresh. I check all the decorations to see that they are in place.

One moment no one is in the house except Busia and I; the next moment the house is filled. Everyone seems to arrive at once, including my mother, who traveled by bus from Detroit and smothers me with hugs, wiping her lipstick kisses from my cheeks with a spit-moistened tissue. All six of Busia's other children and their spouses are here with the cousins, of whom I am the eldest, the automatic leader.

"Merry Christmas!"

"Same to you!"

Enter the relatives, hollering out greetings on the way in. "Happy New Year!" Busia answered. Everyone is carrying presents. It is Christmas Day. The food she prepared is laid out on the kitchen table in holiday dishes on a white linen tablecloth. Auntie Helen and Auntie Mary bring more food, until the table can hold no more. There are ham and coffee cake and rings of kielbasa and stuffed cabbages. Auntie Helen brings mince and pumpkin pies and baked beans. Auntie Della comes bearing cookies and sauerkraut. Auntie Agnes can always be counted on to do or say or bring something weird—this time a green Jell-o mold shimmering with shredded carrots and cabbage. "Good for ya," she says to no one in particular.

Everyone is carrying presents, and I cannot help wondering which are for me. The uncles bring out whiskey, and after they all have "shots," they strut around offering drinks and kisses to all the women and bellow "Merry Christmas and Happy Noooo Year." Before long, they settle down around card tables, with some of the aunts joining the noisy eu-chre and pinochle games.

I take my cousins into the living room and look at the presents. They want to open them right away, but they know they will have to wait. Instead, we play a card game called Go Fish. The younger ones watch. Busia and the aunties are in the kitchen heating up food on the wood stove. Every now and then, we hear shrieks of laughter from Auntie Della when she wins at cards. Uncle Stan tells her to "pipe down." Once in a while, Auntie Agnes fans cigar smoke away from her face and walks into the living room and says, "Whatcha doin'." No one knows who she is talking to, so usually no one answers. Or I say, "playing," and she walks back into the dining room. Uncles Joe and John, the twins, tease everyone and make a lot of noise in Polish. I understand what they are saying, but they don't know it.

Finally, Auntie Helen comes out of the kitchen and says, "All right! Let's eat!"

They let the kids go first. All seven of us rush into the kitchen. Cyn-thia, Margie, and Sandy are old enough to fill their own plates. Auntie Helen fills Cathy's plate. Auntie Louise fills a plate for little Chris and for Uncle Joe. Margie helps her little brother Billy and we all sit around the smaller round table in the corner of the kitchen, while the adults sit at my mother's "Duncanfied" table, which is stretched across the other end of the kitchen.

Soon everyone is eating from plates crammed with ham and sau-sage, beans and potatoes, Jell-o salad, bread, and stuffed cabbages. Then everyone has cake and pie to eat all afternoon. Busia fills and refills plates, sliced ham and cake, and makes sure everyone is eating.

With Christmas tree lights glowing, I turn on the radio in the living room so everyone can eat by Christmas music, though no one really pays much attention.

Finally the time comes when someone says, "Let's open up the presents." From the time those words were spoken until the last present was gone from under the tree, the talking, ripping, and exclaiming do not stop. "Here's something for Margie," Auntie Helen says. And while

Margie goes to get her present, Auntie Mary is saying, "Lennie, look at that! What do you think of that!"

Uncle Hank and Auntie Betty help the cousins unwrap their presents. Then, while Uncle John and Auntie Helen are watching Cynthia and Cathy open their presents. Childless Hank and Betty smile, somehow knowing that their time will come and they will eventually have children of their own.

The whole scene is chaotic, but in the middle of it all I sit near Busia, involved in the pile of presents I have collected, when I hear my name called. I open a small box, which contains a checkered flannel shirt from Uncle Joe and Auntie Louise. I show it to Busia and thank them for it. I open a box from Auntie Agnes and Uncle Harry, which turns out to be a schoolbag. They have no children and everyone seems to know that they never will, although Auntie Agnes will go through at least one "hysterical pregnancy." Calling himself by the name of a TV character he loves, Uncle Harry chirps, "Mr. Peepers thinks you'll be needing that pretty soon." I open a comb and brush set from Uncle Stan and Auntie Della. At the same time, I see Busia open an envelope with a lot of money in it from all her children. Uncle Hank and Auntie Betty give me a clock and tell me I can use it in my own room someday. Uncle John and Auntie Helen, my godparents, give me a Cootie game and tell me it is good for my brain.

Just when I thought I had opened all my presents, Auntie Mary, who has just married a Polish "DP" and would soon join this "displaced person," Uncle Bogdan, in his military career and one day have four children of her own, takes my arm and tells me to look way behind the tree. A huge present is waiting there. "For me?" I ask in disbelief. I pull it out and open it. It is an electric train with a big engine, five cars, and a caboose. Everyone is looking at me, and I try not to show it, but the train is the best gift of all. I can just imagine it set up and running on its own power through my town and around the gas station.

Auntie Mary asks, "Do you like it, Lennie?"

"Oh, yes I do," I say and thank her with a kiss. Busia is watching, and she smiles. "Is very wonderful," she says. My mother stops slicing ham and tells me to open the last box, one that she has lugged all the way from Detroit on the bus. My eyes almost pop out of my head as I unwrap what at first looks like a suitcase but turns out to be a portable record player. Along with it comes my first long-playing album, the RCA Victor recording "60 Years of Music America Loves Best." It is the beginning of my lifelong love for popular music.

Soon all the presents have been opened and the thanks have been said. I pick up the ribbon and wrapping paper that is not too badly torn and put it in a safe place by my bed. Later, after everyone leaves, I will fold it up carefully and put it away for next year.

My cousins and I get together in a corner of the dining room and begin to sing the Christmas songs we all know. We are singing "Jingle Bells" when Auntie Helen joins us. Soon Auntie Mary and Uncle Harry add their voices to the singing. I think it sounds awfully good.

Everyone joins in on "Silent Night," and all of us cousins are surprised at what we have started. Busia is happy. She looks tiny as she rocks in her chair flanked by nightgowns and aprons and slippers and housecoats. She sings along as best she can, for most of the songs she knows are in Polish, and she calls "Silent Night" "*Cicha Noc.*"

So the day passes, until all that is left is a mess to clean up. Christmas is gone. My mother is driven back to the bus station, and Busia and I are alone again. I want the day to go on forever and announce that "it's not over till midnight!" But Christmas is over. We pray hard and silently for the farm that night.

After Christmas, the new year came quickly. We listened to the radio until midnight on New Year's Eve. When the people cheered, I threw confetti I had cut from newspaper. Busia said, "I no can believe is 1954."

Once the new year came, it seemed that winter was on its way out, although there were many more cold mornings to shiver through and many more pails of coal and pieces of wood to bring into the house.

Something strange happens on a day late in February. When Busia announces breakfast, it is as dark outdoors as when we went to bed.

33

Busia says, "Some kind funny weather we have it today." I hurriedly fill the woodbox and bring in some coal. I stick close to the kitchen window, where we can see towers of wildly swirling clouds over the barn. Suddenly a bolt of lightning flashes across the sky, and deafening cracks of thunder shake the house.

Busia switches off the kitchen light. "No sit by a window, lightning strike you," she says, "We sit in dining room."

Busia sits down at her Singer sewing machine and rocks the foot peddle back and forth as she pointlessly sews two pieces of cloth together to give herself something to do.

I try not to look out the window. The clickety-clack of the machine rattles in my ears, but the air outside is so oddly warm and still for a day in February. Thunder shakes the room again.

Busia turns on the radio and tries to find a weather report. There is so much static we can barely understand anything that is being said, except that we should expect "civilian thunderstorms," as she understood it.

"Such a funny business," Busia says. She tries not to show it, but the thunder and lightning frighten her as much as they do me. "Lightning no strike this house. We got it lightning rods on roof," she assures me, ready to accept whatever God has planned for us.

An enormous crash of thunder makes us both wince. In a burst, the lights in the living room go off. So does the radio. Busia says "*Jezus Maria*," then makes the sign of the cross. Through the shadows and out the window, we can see the wind picking up speed. The elm trees along the driveway start to twist, and dead branches break loose and fly away. The wind beats against the walls of the house, making them creak, and building up such power that Busia and I can only stare in wonder.

Busia says quietly, "We go sit in bedroom." We move quickly to Busia's room where she lights the holy candle on her dresser and takes her rosary in her hands. She murmurs prayers, and I try to pray with her, but it is hard for me to keep my eyes from the window, where a sheet of rain beats down from the rumbling dark gray sky.

As quickly as it had risen, the wind stops, and we can hear something hitting the windows. We look out to see what is happening. Hailstones are dropping from the sky, so large that in no time the wet ground is covered with the white marble-like stones.

When the hail stops, it gets very cold. But the sky gets lighter, the electricity comes back on, and Busia and I emerge from the bedroom. A tornado had passed over the house.

I run outside to check out the hailstones. Some are almost as big as robin eggs. I had never seen anything like it and bring one in and put it in the icebox.

For the next week, we talked about the winter thunderstorm. Busia talked to Uncle Hank about it and to Auntie Helen. They both said that they never remembered another one like it. Busia heard on the radio that a "severe" thunderstorm had caused a tornado to pass over the vicinity. Busia kept saying, "Civilian thunderstorms pass it over my vicinity."

Uncle Hank took us down into the basement and showed us where we should go if we had another storm like that one. I hoped we would. The basement was scarier than the attic. It was full of spider webs, dusty jars and baskets, long corridors and stone walls on which the house was built. Uncle Hank finished explaining what we should do in case of another storm, lowering his head to avoid the cobwebs as we climbed the creaky stairs, Uncle Hank asking, "Do you think you can manage if there's ever a tornado?"

My mother had taken me to see *The Wizard of Oz* in Detroit when I was four. I was not at all sure that I could manage, but I nodded "yes."

Later that day, I went out to get more coal, and as I left the coal bin, I saw the landlord's truck in the driveway. He walked slowly back to the porch and reached for the doorknob. "We see, we see," I heard him say. "Don't worry, okay, don't worry about it," he added awkwardly and slipped away.

On wash day, Busia rolled the electric washing machine to the center of the kitchen. It stood like a big white kettle on four legs. She filled it with water she heated on the stove. Connected to the top of the machine were the wringers. Next to the machine on a bench was a wash tub, the same tub I took my baths in. It was filled with ice cold water and a few drops of bluing so that it looked like a clean, fresh little lake.

The machine creaked and churned the clothes rhythmically until they were clean. Then, with the help of her washing stick, Busia lifted them out of the steaming water and put them through the wringer; they landed in the tub of cold water. As I swished the clean clothes around in the tub, Busia put another batch of clothes in the washing machine and closed the cover. Then she put the rinsed clothes back through the wringer, and I caught them as they landed on the cover and threw them into the clothes basket—an old bushel basket with oilcloth.

Even in cold weather, Busia liked to hang the wet clothes on the line in the yard, where sometimes they would freeze stiff as boards. The next day, she would iron dresses and doilies and shirts and aprons with a flat iron that required no electricity but was heated by sitting on the kitchen wood stove until it sizzled when it made contact with a shot of water.

In the middle of our work, Busia glances out the window above the kitchen sink. "Oh, here come crazy man," she says in Polish and runs to the porch window, where the washing machine can be seen from outside, and closes the curtains. She hurries to the back door, locks it, and makes a beeline to the radio and switches it off. Then she turns off the washing machine and grabs my arm.

"Come, we hide behind stove." We cower in the sheltered spot where I take my baths. "Oh, I forget," Busia says and darts into the dining room and locks the side door. She hurries back to my side. "Now *cicho*," she tells me, "No say word."

By this time, a beat-up green truck has pulled into the driveway and stopped in the back yard. A man wearing a wool vest steps out, walks up the steps to the porch, and knocks on the door. We are petrified and only Busia knows why.

"I not like this peddler," Busia whispers as she stares at the door. Everything is quiet except for the stranger's pounding.

I remembered the last time the peddler came. He was a short, bald man who spoke peculiar English. He talked and talked, and I remembered how desperately Busia had tried to get rid of him, but she did not know how to say no. He talked her into buying a bottle-washing brush, a bar of tar soap, and a strainer. She was angry after he finally left. How could he have talked her in to all those things?

The knocking finally stops, and the truck pulls away. The peddler has given up.

Busia sighs and begins to undo her precautions. She laughs as she turns the washing machine back on. "Funny business, no?" she says to me.

"Why don't you like him?" I ask.

"I no can get rid of it him. He trick me and I spend money."

I did not understand, but I rather enjoyed sneaking behind the stove, and I hoped the peddler would come again.

Spring

April brings Easter, and to my way of thinking, the most important thing about Easter is coloring eggs. On Good Friday, Busia takes a pot off the shelf above the stove, adds water, and settles it on a burner to boil. The pot contains onion skins that she has soaked overnight. Now we are ready for the coloring to begin.

Busia cleans and washes three dozen eggs. There are to be four colors. The onion skins will make one color, a pot of beet juice another, chopped bark from one of the oak logs in the garage another, and yet another will come from the husks of walnuts that we picked up from the ground around the walnut tree and stored in a bushel basket in the garage. I am removing the pulp that surrounds the nut. The pulp will make the dye, and I will have plenty of work to do trying to crack open the nut and pick out the meat. Busia has four small pots on the stove, which contain the four different colors soaked in water and vinegar. She places nine eggs in each pot and brings them all to a boil. They remain there until they are hard-boiled. At the same time, the eggs absorb color. The ones in the onion skin dye come out bright orange; the ones in the beet dye a delicate pink; the ones in the oak bark turn pale yellow; and the ones in the walnut pulp are chocolaty brown.

After Busia takes the eggs out of the pots, she places them on the cooling rack, which I have fashioned with scissors out of Uncle John's old egg cartons. I watch the whole procedure carefully. Once the eggs on the rack are cool and dry, I pick up each one, examine it, and place it in a bowl of straw.

In a couple of hours the eggs have all been brightly colored and stacked in two bowls on the kitchen table. Busia is busy cleaning up the mess so she can be ready for church when Uncle Hank comes for us. Good Friday was a very important day, a day to be quiet, to pray, and to contemplate what it means to die for love. From twelve noon until three o'clock, we will be in church praying the "Stations of the Cross" and watching the priest and altar boys go through their holy rituals. Busia takes her Polish prayer book and her rosary and murmurs prayers through the entire service.

All the statues in the church are shrouded in purple, the color of mourning, and the church is filled with the smoke of incense. The priests chant in Latin, and the people kneel and stand, kneel and stand, over and over again. Near the end of the three hours, the congregation files to the front of the church to kiss the cross, which is nestled on a pillow at the foot of the altar. One by one, all the parishioners get down on their hands and knees and kiss the feet of the bloodied and nearly naked figure on the cross. An altar boy wipes the statue after each kiss.

I dread the whole display. Busia goes first. She kneels and bows her head down to the feet of Christ where she places her lips. She makes the sign of the cross. Then it is my turn. I do what Busia has done, quickly, and dash off behind her to our pew. Then everyone leaves the church except those who want to go to confession. Busia and Uncle Hank stay. I watch them preparing to tell the priest their sins. What did Busia do wrong? I wondered, and what will I tell the priest when I make my First Holy Communion?

Easter morning is the time to shake off the sadness of Good Friday, to rejoice in new life that resurrects from the cold ground in spring. I awaken to tantalizing smells coming from the kitchen. An Easter ham is in the oven. Busia presents me with an Easter basket containing chocolate eggs, a chocolate bunny, marshmallow chicks, and jelly beans that always fall to the bottom of the paper grass where they can be found in the days ahead.

Busia places her coffee cake and the colored eggs on the table. I try to help her prepare for the visits from her children.

"Happy Easter. How is good day?" says Busia. "Smile and world smile with you. Cry, you cry alone."

The month of April was unusually dry. I was digging in a flower bed at the side of the house, across the driveway, where huge rose bushes were overgrown with runners that never had flowers on them. I cut some of them away and raked leaves off the spots where tiny tulip and crocus buds were just starting to appear.

Separated from the yard by a rickety fence was a small field, which used to be a strawberry patch. A few strawberries still showed up there every now and then. The little field also contained a cherry tree with some currant and gooseberry bushes beneath it, two large pear trees, a grapevine, and lots of little elm trees that had sprouted up in the untilled soil because of the row of large elm trees nearby. The little field was separated by a row of peach trees from the big fields, which reached back to the creek.

When I got tired of raking, I went into the little field and looked around for signs of spring in the matted dry grass. Having conquered the cherry tree last year, I climbed the pear tree. I found plenty of low branches and pulled myself nearly to the top. It was covered with buds, and from my perch I could see Busia through the kitchen window. I could also see a car speeding down the road, and I could almost see the creek.

I went back to work, raking and thinking about how great it would be if I could somehow make the little field into part of the lawn. I figured that with so many important trees and shrubs in it, the lawn addition would give Uncle Harry more grass to mow. I was sure he would be grateful.

I got a bright idea: I know! Other people burned off land, and when the new grass came up there was no old grass in its way. When grass grows where land has been burned, it becomes a blanket of short green sprouts, smooth as any lawn. I had seen it many times down along the road.

I run to the house, dash into the pantry, and shove a box of wooden matches into my pocket.

"You work hard? Pretty soon dinner," Busia calls, as I fly past her.

"I'm fixing the yard," I reply and head out the door toward a corner of the little field near the road. I pile the leaves and grass that I had raked away from the roses onto the dry grass.

A breeze blows out my first match. But the second match lights the pile and sets some of the grass on fire. I figure that I will use my rake to guide and control the fire. The little flames spread quickly and head outward. They eat up the dead grass like flickering tongues and leave a charred trail.

I decide I should start putting some of the fire out because it is going in so many directions. I let part of it go toward the ditch, since it will be stopped by the road. I am trying to beat out some of the fire that is headed toward the lawn. I beat at it with the rake, but it flares up again. I step on some of the tiny flames that are gobbling grass, but now the rest of the fire is spreading fast, back toward the peach trees.

I run to the house to get something larger to beat with. Out of breath as I push myself onto the porch, I grab the floor mop drying there and run back to the field. The flames are crossing the little field, which now seems enormous. I beat them until the mop is scorched and singed, and still the flames spread. The line of moving fire grows wider and longer, and the black area grows larger.

"*Mój Boże*!" Busia screams from the porch. "Oh my God!" Hands on her head, she runs to the field with an old rug, saying nothing more, only beating out flames as quickly as she can. I run to the house again and grab a bucket and fill it with water from the outdoor pump. I dunk the mop in it and beat out more flames. My chest hurts, but I keep beating, harder and harder as my breathing grows heavier. I look over at Busia frantically beating the flames, which are heading for the end of the little field where the corn cribs and the barn stand waiting.

Just then, I see two men walking toward us from the road. Their car is parked where the gravel driveway has stopped the fire. They say nothing but grab the mop from me and tell me to get more water and something else to beat with. I force myself to run to the house again and get another porch rug. Panting, I grab the shovel and run back.

The men are efficient. When they hit the flames, they do not flare up again. In a short time, they extinguish the fire, just as it seems beyond control. They speak a few words to Busia, who manages a stunned thank-you. The men get in their car and disappear down the road. I look over the black little field. A couple of fence posts are still smoldering at their bases. Busia pours water on them. The fire has stopped only inches from the first corn crib, and as I look past the row of peach trees, I realize there was nothing to stop the fire for as far as I can see. The whole big field and the neighbor's field, as well as all our houses, might have burned.

I walk silently to the porch and sit on the steps, watching Busia check every last smoking spot. She picks up the mop and rugs, which are ruined, and brings them up to the porch. As she lays them down, shaking her head, she comes as close to scolding as she ever has: "I go lay down. You fix it yard good."

I look at Busia's eyes; they are wet with tears. Her hand is shaking as she reaches for a chair to support herself. I want to say I am sorry, but I can only stare at Busia as she walks to her bedroom.

I stand still for a while then follow Busia into her room. She is lying on her back, staring. I follow her gaze to the discolored ceiling paper, then I look down at her. "We don't have to go away now, do we?" I ask.

"We no go no place," she says. Then she laughs, "Maybe we go to Armada buy it new mop."

It is spring, a sunny day. Busia pulls down all the heavy drapes and opens the living room and parlor to welcome the warm weather. She decides one morning that it is time to work in the garden, behind the old chicken coop.

We head for the garage. Busia is wearing her tattered straw hat. She selects a shovel and a rake. "You bring *motyka*. That's it," she instructs.

I follow with the hoe as we walk through the new grass, past the pile of tree limbs, past the chicken coop. Busia goes right to work, no doubt remembering that not so many years ago a successful garden, along with chickens and milk cows, was the only thing that kept her children from going hungry during the long Michigan winters.

"Is be lots work. Dirt good today." The ground is not too dry and not too wet. Busia puts her shovel into position and forces it into the ground with her foot. She turns the shovelful upside down. I move in next to her and begin chopping at the newly exposed earth with my hoe. We work for a couple of hours, taking our time and talking about what we will plant.

Then we walk back to the house for lunch, which Busia called dinner. She called the evening meal supper and told me not to "eat over." I was what my mother called "a picky eater." I liked dry tuna fish out of a can on dry bread, no oil, no mayonnaise. I liked mashed potatoes and sauerkraut, mixed together. My mother tried to make chop suey on one of her visits from the city. She was an adventurous eater. I refused to eat it. "If you were starving you'd eat it," she told me. On such occasions, Busia usually placed some bread and butter or some tuna fish in front of me. I would beg for a hot dog or its Polish counterpart *serdelki*, which my mother would now and then bring from the city along with day-old bread that she could buy for a few cents.

After her nap, Busia says it is time to go back out to the garden and work for a couple more hours.

By three o'clock, we have dug up a good-sized piece of land. It is big enough for our purposes, anyway. We would plant only a few things—things that the aunts and uncles didn't bring us. "Oh, Ma," Uncle Hank would say when Busia asked him to come over with his tractor and plow up her garden, "You don't have to plant a garden anymore."

The next day, the little garden is ready to be raked. We work the ground until it is smooth. As we take turns hoeing and raking, Busia explains that the big wooden rake was made by Dziadzia, and in the old days such rakes were used to put hay and straw into rows to be picked up and formed into haystacks, food for the cows.

When the ground is prepared, we stretch garden cord from one end of the plot to the other. Busia directs me, and when the line of cord looks straight, she instructs me to put my stake in the ground. We plant seeds alongside the cord so the rows will be straight.

After supper, Busia brings out six tiny tomato plants, which she has grown from seeds in little clay pots on the kitchen window sill. She also brings out some potatoes that have begun sprouting in the pantry and cuts them into pieces, making sure there is at least one "eye" on each piece. In the garden plot we had room for one row each of radishes, beets, carrots, lettuce, green beans, and a row each of sweet corn and popcorn. They were short rows, planted from the packages of seeds that Busia bought on her trips to town with Auntie Helen. Busia went to town once a month to buy things for the pantry: rice, flour, sugar. In the pantry she also kept the jars of peaches and pears that she put up for the winter. Ice for the icebox was delivered by the iceman, coffee by the coffee man, bread and other treats by the bakery man. Eggs and chickens she got from Uncle John or Uncle Stan or from the little market within walking distance of the house. Uncle Hank brought milk from his cows, and Busia churned butter in a big glass churn with a crank on top and paddles inside.

Only once did I ever see Busia pluck a chicken. She did it on the porch because the odor was horrible. When she brought the chicken into the kitchen to get it ready to cook, she found that it was full of eggs. "*Oy yoy yoy.* Wrong chicken," she said.

When we are finished in the garden, we walk back to the house, but before we get to the back porch, we see a car pulling into the driveway. It is the landlord, this time with one of his sons. I learn later that they came to tell Busia they want her to have a telephone.

"He say me is cost only little bit every month. Is be nice for me, and he need it telephone in summer they work here." There were to be some changes on the farm. The landlord had talked to Busia about a bathroom and a furnace. He had many changes planned, and they were to be done before the next winter.

In the middle of the afternoon, Busia walks out of the house carrying her garden scissors. "I gonna pick it some lilac," she says.

I run behind Busia as she heads down the driveway. The lilac bushes are covered with huge lavender flowers, and the fragrance fills the air. I run behind Busia as she heads down the driveway. There is a lilac bush in each corner of the front yard, and there are two smaller ones in the side yard. We pick bunches of the flowers carefully so as not to leave bare spots on any of the bushes.

Busia snips blossoms and hands them to me as I stand sniffing and exclaiming about how good they smell. "Very good, very sweet, very nice," she says, reaching for a lofty stem, "Very fine."

Just as we finish picking as many lilacs as my arms can hold, a big truck with Michigan Bell Telephone printed on its side pulls into the driveway. Busia goes to meet it while I take the lilacs to the house.

For the rest of the afternoon, I watch men take over the dining room, drilling and running wires out to the porch and up the side of the house. Then they connect the house to a telephone pole with a thick wire that stretches over the front yard.

Busia instructs me to watch the supper on the kitchen stove as the men explain to her how to dial the telephone. They tell her about the party line she shares with unidentified neighbors, and they tell her three short rings mean the phone call is for her and not somebody else.

"Very good," she says, "and thank you very much." As she leads the telephone men to the door, they explain that she will get a bill for two dollars plus "long distance" charges at the end of the month. And they tell her to dial zero for the operator if she has any trouble.

"Maybe I call Auntie Helen," Busia decides. She picks up the receiver and holds it delicately to her ear. Cautiously she dials the number her daughter-in-law has given her, handling the phone as if it is an object from another planet, unaware that before we are through with the black magic novelty it will have dropped to the floor numerous times on its way to becoming an essential part of our lives.

I stand very close, but everything is silent. Then I hear the faint voice of my godmother at the other end of the line saying, "Hello."

Busia shouts into the phone, "Hello! Who is calling!"

I can hear Auntie Helen laughing through the receiver. "*You* are calling, Ma, *you* are calling."

"I no think I like it this telephone," Busia decides.

Next to the little field that I had burned was a row of elm trees. During colder months the rope in the barn was good for swinging. But in the warm weather, I wanted to be outdoors. One time when Uncle Harry came over to mow the lawn with his new power mower, he brought a long hemp rope with him. He fetched a step ladder from the garage and stood on it, looking at each of the elms.

Uncle Harry selected an elm near the pump house, and he put the ladder under a low branch that stuck out straight and strong over the lawn. He tied the rope securely to the limb. Then he cut the rope and tied the new piece to the same limb. He did that again, so there were three pieces of rope dangling to the ground.

Uncle Harry knew about the pile of old tires behind the chicken coop. I watched every move. Uncle Harry rolled an old tire out from behind the weeds and old farm machinery and toward the elm tree. I could hear water sloshing around in the tire. It was smelly rain water. When we got back to the ropes, Uncle Harry bounced and flipped the tire to get the water out. It is very difficult to get water out of an old tire.

Finally Uncle Harry secured the tire to the ropes, parallel to the ground. The tire swing was finished.

"Go ahead and try it, Lennie," he said.

I stretched across the tire and gave myself a shove with my feet. It was great. I didn't even have to hang on to the ropes. I could lie back and look up through the elm leaves at the sky. I knew right then that I would never tire of the tire swing and would spend hours suspended there, staring up at the sky through the tree branches. But the trees got Dutch elm disease and Uncle Hank had to cut them all down.

Summer

During the warm days of summer, I often walked down the lane behind the barn to the creek. The lane was two tracks made by years of wheels traveling from the barn to the creek and over the wooden bridge to fields beyond. The lane was like a road except that weeds grew tall on either side of it, and they were beginning to grow taller down the center because there were no cows to chew them down on their way to the moist grassy pasture on either side of the creek.

Some days I could go to the edge of our farm and see Uncle Joe's cows. They would amble up to the fence, which was a thin electric wire, and stare at me. I could see their teeth as they chewed their cud. They were always chewing; some would stand in the middle of the creek. The cows never touched the electric fence. They seemed to know exactly how close they could come without getting a poke. The cows were lumbering and gentle. Nothing ever seemed to upset them. They only rolled their huge eyes and kept chewing. Sometimes I would be at the creek when Uncle Joe was yelling "ka-baas" from his barn. The cows all turned from what they were doing and headed toward their own lane, which led to their own barn, where it was time for milking.

One warm day, I ask Busia if I can go down to the creek. It is the kind of summer day when everything moves more slowly than usual. I take my time too, examining all the things along the lane: the rocks, the ant hills, the crabapple tree, the berry bushes heavy with red-green berries, and the willow trees.

When I finally reach the creek, I feel as though I could stay there forever. The water is always moving, always going somewhere. I start at the bridge and walk alongside the creek on the paths that cows have made—when there were cows on the farm. They had walked as close to the water as they could without falling in. Sometimes the paths are so close to the edge that I have trouble with my balance and wonder how the cows had managed with their bovine selves.

In some places the water is shallow, and it ripples as it travels over rocks. In other spots it looks quite deep and seems still, even though it is moving. Short bushy willow trees grow on the creek banks, almost in the water. I lean on them to get a better look.

I walk along the creek to the end of the farm and find a narrow part of the creek where I jump across. Near the neighbors' land to the east is a grove where wild, reed-like willows grow so close together no grass grows on the ground beneath them. The grove is like a little jungle. Though I can see where the grove ends, I walk to the middle of it, and there it seems as if I am in a dense forest. A tiny tributary of the creek runs through the center of the grove. It has water in it only during very wet weather. It is now a dry ditch, and I walk through it.

As I walk back to the bridge, a muskrat swims by, frogs leap into the creek, and pheasants fly up in front of me without warning, making my heart skip a beat. The bridge is made of wood—two huge logs laid across the creek, with planks nailed to them. At one time it must have been very strong, but it is beginning to rot. I lie on my stomach with my head hanging over the edge and gaze into the center of the creek. It is busy with fish—tiny minnows, swimming and sucking in water. They dart about, and I can make them move simply by waving my hand over the water. I throw a pebble into the stream and watch the fish scurry away. Gradually they all come back, curious to see if anything new has arrived for them to eat. Every once in a while a crab crawls out from the weedy banks and looks around, clicking its pincers.

The water is shallow by the bridge, and the day is very hot, so I take off my shoes and socks, roll up my pant legs, and splash the water with my feet. It feels so good that soon I am standing almost knee deep in the creek. The bottom is sandy, and I reach down and examine a handful.

Tiny clams inhabit the creek bottom; I scoop a handful of sand onto the bridge and pry their shells open to expose the shiny gluey mass within. I throw some of the other tiny clams into the water, and they dig their way back into the creek bottom. Part of the creek bank by the bridge is lower than the rest of the bank and juts out into the water. I hop over to it, like leaping onto a little grassy island.

A plan develops. If I could dig out the small area that connects the peninsula to the bank, it would be an island, only a few feet long, but nevertheless an island. I find a big stick, and with my hands and feet dig out the connection. As I dig, the water clouds up with mud. When the mud clears, the land is surrounded by water.

I slop around in the water for a while, marveling at my engineering feat, before I hear Busia's voice calling me home: "Lenuś! *Czas do domu.*" I jump back onto the bridge, pick up my shoes and socks, and head up the lane toward home. I notice what looks like pieces of mud stuck to my ankles. I brush at them, but they still stick. I pick one piece and pull it off, but it is slimy and not crumbly the way drying mud usually is. When I see blood running down my leg, I realize that the "mud" is alive—leeches! I pull the other one off and throw it as hard as I can. Then I jump up and down at the thought of holding that fat blood-bloated little body between my fingers. Two tiny red streams are running down my leg all the way to my foot as I head up the lane. What else can I do but wipe them off with my hand and wipe my hand on my pants?

I walk back up the lane toward home, thinking about Dziadzia's weeping willow trees and their thousands of sinewy branches bent toward the ground. There were five large trees along the lane. The smallest was near the beginning of the pasture near the creek, and they got gradually larger up to the barn. The largest was twenty or thirty feet high and nearly as wide. The weeping willows had been planted by Dziadzia many years before he died, and he used the pliable switches to make baskets used for potato picking. Everything on the farm belonged to Busia and Dziadzia, I thought.

As I approach the final willow tree, I stop to inspect it, opening the curtain of branches and stepping beneath the tree. It is like a room with leafy walls and a rough black chimney in the center. Looking up, I see the network of branches that had not been visible from the outside. I pull off a small branch and swat the ground with it, remembering how we had used willow branches to roast hot dogs last summer. Willow branches were so useful.

In a flash, I am onto another bright idea. "I know!" I rush out from under the tree and run up the lane, around the barn. Busia is sweeping off the back porch, carefully avoiding the bees nest in the roof above her. She looks up at me.

"You no hear me call you before? I think maybe you get it lost," she yells.

"I need my wagon," I yell back, headed for the garage to get my beat-up Radio Flyer. It was pretty old and didn't look like much; it had done a lot of hauling in its day. "I'll be right back," I call. "I'm just gonna go get some willow branches."

"Pretty soon supper," Busia calls after me as she takes off her straw hat and shakes her head. I pull my wagon back to the big willow tree, break off branches, and pile a great heap of them on the wagon without even leaving a noticeable bare spot in the veil of branches.

My idea is going to take shape in the yard behind the garage and it requires the two porch chairs from the side of the house that Busia sat on when she plucked the pheasants her son brought her after they went hunting or to grind horseradish she dug up along the fence. I find some boards in the garage, which I lay across the backs of the chairs, making a roof from chair to chair. Then I lay willow branches over the frame made by the chairs and the boards.

It takes two trips back to the willow tree in the lane, but finally I have constructed what looks like a grass hut. The willow branches completely hide the boards and the chairs. A great hideout with plenty of room inside.

I left it in the back yard for many days, until the willow branches were dry and brown. It turned out to be a great place to talk to my cousins or to cool off or to sort rocks for my rock collection. I would build many more of them before I was through.

In August there were many vegetables and fruits to be picked, each ripening in its own time. Busia told stories of working in fields all day long when she was a young girl in Poland and from dawn to dusk in the fields of Michigan where she and Dziadzia harvested vegetables and fruit as tenant farmers, working for a share of the crops instead of wages. She recalled a time when they had knelt in the fields and prayed for rain.

Blackberries ripen early in the season, and today is the day to pick them. Busia and I find two small pails in the pantry and set off for the fields beyond the creek. Around each field and into the woods are bush after bush of blackberries, each branch loaded with shiny, plump fruit. I start picking berries faster than my hands can move and eating just about every third berry. Once in a while Busia pops some into her mouth too. They are delicious. And they grow wild. No one planted them. No one took care of them.

The days that follow berry picking are days for canning. Busia makes blackberry jam and blackberry pie and tells me, her Lenuś, to go to the little field beside the house and pick the ripe currants and gooseberries. Under the cherry tree and pear trees there are enough currant and goose-berry bushes to provide berries for quite a few jars of jam; I pick and pick until my pail is full of the sour little berries. While picking, I notice that many of the cherries have already turned bright red. Why hadn't Busia asked me to pick those as well? No matter, I reach up to the lower branches and eat some of the tangy cherries, spitting the pit on the ground.

When I have eaten enough cherries, I take another full pail of gooseberries into the house where Busia is standing over the steaming stove making dill pickles from the bushel of pickles Auntie Helen had brought over.

"Here's the gooseberries," I announce, "And guess what! The cherries were ripe too, and I ate a whole bunch of them! They're sour."

"*Oy yoy oy*! I hope you not eat too many. You should ask me first."

"What's the matter? What did I do?" I am surprised at Busia's reaction. She puts down her funnel and leads me across the driveway to the cherry tree.

"Let I show it you," Busia says, plucking a ripe cherry from the tree. She breaks it open and exposes the juicy center. "You see this," she says.

I look closely, and there, near the pit is a tiny segmented green worm crawling in the juicy fruit. I groan, suddenly feeling quite sick.

Busia picks cherry after cherry and exposes a worm in each. "They all have worms just about if you no spray them," she says.

We walk back to the house, I thinking for sure that I will throw up but talking myself out of it because that would mean I would have to see those little green worms again!

"Little bit meat before supper no hurt you," Busia teases.

After that, I was very careful with the rest of our crops. But when the carrots got big enough, I went out to the garden, pulled one up, wiped it off on my pants, and ate it. It was worm free. All the garden crops were close to being ready for picking. More and more green beans started ripening. We picked a big bowlful every third day, and when there were enough, Busia canned them. All through August, garden vegetables ripened. The aunts and uncles brought over bushels of tomatoes and corn. It kept Busia and me very busy.

During that same month, visits from the landlord and his sons were common. They dug up the flower garden beneath the kitchen window and ran a pipe across the driveway to the new well being dug by a drill rig on the back of an enormous truck. Inside the house, there was a new porcelain sink, which replaced the pump and tub-like old sink. I stayed out of the way of the workmen most of the time, but I did try to move some of the flowers out of their way before the men started digging the pipeline.

"They're digging everything up!" I ran into the house hollering on the day before my seventh birthday.

"Good, good, everything is good," Busia replied.

My birthday was a warmer-than-average summer day: August 25. The sun was blazing but a cool breeze was flowing over the farm. The trees whispered as they moved with the wind. I was watching the workmen as they walked in and out of the house trying to get the new plumbing to operate.

My mother made a special trip from Hamtramck to bring my birthday present. "Do you like it?" she asks, as she presents me with records by Patti Page, Perry Como, and the Mills Brothers. My mother says, "Now maybe you will stop pestering Grandma and asking 'What should I do?' all the time."

Just then I get an idea: "I know!" I run into the living room where Busia is sitting in the overstuffed brown easy chair, resting and listening to the men working outside.

Many times, I had walked with Busia to the little market down the road, and many times she and I had been driven there by one of the aunties. Today, I have decided I am now old enough to walk from the farm to the little corner store all alone.

I squeeze into the chair next to Busia to get ready for the big ask. She moves to make room, but she does not open her eyes. I wait. And wait. I twist and cough a bit to get her attention. Finally I can hold back no more, "Busia, if I ask you will you let me do something important today? It's my birthday. I'm seven years old now, and I have to go to school, and I want to know if I can walk to the store by myself."

"*Oy yoy oy*, you want to walk it by you self?" she laughs. "Well I no know. Cars drive it like crazy. Somebody maybe pick you up...."

"Oh Busia, please," I beg, "I'll watch for cars, and I'll look before I cross. I walk to the creek alone. Please. Why can't I go? Please?"

"I no chew my cabbage twice," says Busia.

"Oh please can I go? It's my birthday." I beg until my mother says, "Quit pestering Grandma."

"Mama, maybe you need me to buy something for you?" I bargain.

"Okay, all right, buy me a pound of hamburger and half a gallon of milk," she answers, puffing on a Pall Mall, "oh, and two packs of cigarettes." She takes two dollars out of her purse.

"Put in you pocket," Busia says, as I head for the door.

"And buy yourself some candy with the change," my mother adds, "and look both ways before you cross Thirty-two."

"Take it easy. No rush. God bless you," Busia calls after me as I run down the driveway to the road, look back and wave. She and my mother, side by side, smile and wave. Busia looks a little worried. I am giddy over having convinced them to let me go.

The store is about a quarter of a mile down 32 Mile Road. But the walk seems short. I pass the neighbors' houses. Next to me, the ditches look like small versions of the creek, but filled with cattails. There are bottles lying along the road and a dead sparrow that must have been hit by a car. Thinking about the dead bird, I am surprised when I arrive at the store so quickly.

Inside the store, the owner looks at me and asks what I want. He brings the milk and hamburger to the counter, pulls two packs of cigarettes off the rack, and announces that it will all cost one dollar and fifteen cents. Then I begin picking out penny candies, eighty-five of them. There are so many kinds it is hard to choose, but I like the wax bottles full of sweet syrup and the watermelon slices and the candy dots on paper. I spend every penny of the change on candy, ending up with a bagful.

"What else can I get for you today, young man?" The owner speaks with an accent that isn't Polish. Busia said the man spoke Ukrainian.

I pay the owner two dollars and say good-bye as I leave the Cloverleaf Market. "Good-bye," says the old man, smiling.

When I get home, Busia and my mother are waiting. There is a cake on the table with seven candles on it. "Happy Birthday Day!" Busia says.

"What's in that sack?" my mother asks, as I show her the bag I was able to fill with penny candy. "What?" she scolds. "I told you to buy a few pieces with the change, not spend all my money on candy." She promptly picks up the phone and calls the Cloverleaf Market. "No, I did not tell him to bring home a bag of candy. No, you should know better. Yes, I want him to take it back." And my mother and I march back to the store for a refund on all but a few pieces of the candy. "Well you told me to buy candy with the change," I protest. "Don't be ridiculous," she says. "Do I look like I'm made of money? That candy is no good for you anyway."

My birthday went by quietly. Uncle John and Auntie Helen, my godparents, came over for cake with Cynthia and Cathy. They brought me a new pair of cotton pajamas. My mother also gave me two new coloring books, and Busia gave me a box of crayons. "You like it to draw, no?" she said. They were wonderful coloring books, the kind with real-looking people, with all the right details to fill in.

Twelve days later, Busia's birthday came. I gave her a dish towel that I bought on my second trip to the little market alone. Busia's children stopped by during the week and brought her cards with money in them. And so Busia's birthday also passed by, with me memorizing the words to "How Much Is That Doggie in the Window" and "Glow Worm."

One night in August as Busia and I were eating supper, the telephone rang. Busia hurried into the dining room and awkwardly lifted the receiver to her ear. She stood for a long time nodding and saying "yah" and "no" and glancing at me. Then she said "Thank-you" and "very good, very nice" and hung up. She walked back to the table and, said, "We gonna pay it five dollar bigger rent!"

I knew that meant for sure that we would not have to move. The landlord had called to say that he would continue to rent the house to us and rent the land to somebody else. The news warranted big hugs. I buried my face in Busia's apron. I knew even then that she could not promise me that we would stay forever, but still I wanted to hear it. "Everything is good, everything is fine, everything is nice, Lenuś," Busia assured me, with her hand stroking my hair.

The landlord and his sons were fast workers who seemed to know how to build or repair just about anything. They completed nearly all the planned changes before summer was over. They had taken all the old brown wooden cupboards out of the pantry, and every day the room began to look more and more like a bathroom. The men were busy for a while in the basement laying new pipes. Then they worked in the pantry installing the bathtub, sink, and toilet. Then they worked in the basement again while Busia and I rearranged all the canning and pots and pans on shelves away from the pipes.

And so the men went back and forth until the bathroom was finished and the pantry roughly rebuilt in the tiny area beneath the stairs to the second floor, next to the rickety stairs to the basement. Then we brought all the jars back upstairs.

When they had finished these changes, the landlord and his sons did not come again for a week. We had time to be alone with the new fixtures, and I loved the changes. Busia fussed and protested as though she did not deserve such conveniences.

"I no know how use these things. Maybe I no like it," she complained when she had trouble closing the bathtub drain. I reminded her that everything would be so easy from now on. Busia really knew that it was time for the farm to have a bathroom and a kitchen sink. We were far behind other people. She knew that the extra work caused by the lack of these "luxuries" was unnecessary. And so she accepted all the new contraptions. She had no choice, anyway. She had seen her children in their own homes, installing these conveniences. Uncle Hank built his own modern ranch-style house almost ten miles away. Uncle John built new cupboards and installed a bathroom in his farmhouse on Pitt Road. Uncle Stan lived past Richmond near land that would become Interstate 94, a place where I and my cousins could play on weekends in the overpass under construction. Uncle Joe would eventually sell the farm next door and move to a bigger and more remote farm in Croswell, where he could work more land and milk more cows in a barn that seemed larger than an airplane hangar.

I explored the half-basement beneath the kitchen and inspected the new pump and the pipes leading up to the bathroom and kitchen. The new pump changed the forbidding appearance of the dirt floors and low ceilings covered with cobwebs.

Near the beginning of September, the landlord and his sons came again. This time, they brought bags of cement and a cement mixer. They hauled in a truckload of gravel, which they dumped in the driveway between the back porch and the garage and started work on a new chimney. They began in the basement where the furnace would go.

The chimney shot up through the dining room. The landlord's sons cut holes in the dining room floor and in the floor in the bedroom above. The chimney grew quickly, and soon the men were on the roof building the last of it. I spent most of the day watching the men work. They almost never spoke to me, but they didn't seem to mind my being there.

The chimney shot up through the center of the house, huge and made of new bricks. It rose in front of the door to the attic and now it was hard for me to squeeze in. A new furnace soon followed, installed in a day by a crew of men working in the basement. I didn't watch them work. I would have been in the way. Besides, there were things to be picked in the garden, and the creek was a shallow trickle fine for wading and leaping across.

I came in the house to find that registers had been installed in every room to let in the heat from the furnace. The landlord and his sons loaded the wood stoves onto their truck and took them to the dump. Auntie Mary bought Busia a new electric stove and refrigerator with money from her new job in Richmond. It all happened so quickly.

Busia fussed about the new stove and had a terrible time learning how to use it. All the English words on the stove, like "moderate," didn't mean to much to her. Auntie Mary told her laughingly not to try to build a fire in the oven.

The landlord came once a month for his rent, and we stared at him suspiciously until he left, but he never mentioned changing his mind.

There were so many changes that summer that Busia and I did not know what to make of them. The cement mixer in the yard kept turning through September, making cement for new porches. The landlord even got rid of the bees nest in the back porch eaves—but not before one of the evicted tenants stung me on the ear.

I tried to move all the irises and tulips out of the way of the work, but when school started I was too preoccupied to move them all, so many of them got trampled.

I was the oldest and tallest student in my first-grade class and bewildered by the new routines and instructions I was expected to follow.

Busia stayed home alone all day now. She waited for me to come home on the bus, and then she would ask me about what I had learned.

The coming winter would be different with no fires to keep going, no cold walks to the outdoor toilet with bags of lime. Busia would have more time for herself, to bake and sew and work on her hooked rugs in her rocking chair.

Tractors pulled in and out of the driveway regularly as the neighboring farmers plowed the weeds under and worked the soil. They headed down the lane pulling cultivators and discs. I watched them disappear past the willows, where Busia and I continued to walk each winter for seven more years, until the row of Christmas trees in the meadow was gone.

Afterword

While the events and people portrayed in this book are drawn from memory, many details have been invented or fictionalized for the sake of the story. Some events are composites of actual events that took place at different times. I owe a debt of thanks to my cousins who continue to share their memories of Busia with me. Thanks also to my friend and colleague Louise Kertesz for her careful reading and editing of the manuscript. I also want to thank Wayne State University for long ago giving me a Tompkins Award for an early version of this story, which gave me the confidence to resurrect and rewrite it.